The Passionate Practitioner's Handbook

Love
Michelle xx

THE PASSIONATE PRACTITIONER'S HANDBOOK

The book information is catalogued as follows;

Author Name(s): Michele Doull & Avril Robertson

THE PASSIONATE PRACTITIONER'S HANDBOOK

Description: First Edition

Book Design by Lynda Mangoro

ISBN: 978-1-914447-34-1

Prepared by That Guy's House Ltd.

www.ThatGuysHouse.com

The Passionate Practitioner's Handbook

How to Transform and Inspire Your Early Years Practice

Michele Doull   Avril Robertson

About the Authors

Michele Doull changed career 17 years ago and began a journey to understand and appreciate the needs of our youngest children and the adults who work tirelessly with and for them. Getting it right for both children and adults drives Michele's professional practice and she is committed to encouraging adults to truly hear the voice of children; listening for the words that are felt but perhaps not able to be spoken.

Michele is a mum to two amazing sons and she and her husband live in Central Scotland.

Avril Robertson is an early years consultant with over 35 years' experience working in the early education sector. She is passionate about presenting information to all within the early years workforce in ways that are relevant, engaging and based on real experiences.

Avril lives in Central Scotland with her lovely husband Steven and is the mother of three, awesome (triplet) sons.

Forewords

Jean Carwood-Edwards
Professional Adviser to Scottish Government

What I love about this beautiful book is that the authors write from the heart, showing their deep connection with, and understanding of, the role of the early years professional.

The tone and the key messages within this handbook take careful account of the realities of everyday life in an early years setting. This is a book that says it as it is!

Tackling complex issues with simple language and jargon-free honesty makes the book invaluable for students, newly qualified staff, and experienced professionals.

Whilst fully fledged qualified practitioners will recognise themselves in the narrative and enjoy the invitation to re-visit and reflect on their own perspectives about their work, students are offered an invaluable opportunity to gain an authentic insight into the world of early years.

The authors have a very natural, conversational style which I found to be both compelling and easy to read. I particularly like the way in which the authors speak directly to the readers throughout the book, almost as if they are engaging the reader in professional dialogue in the staff room!

I also thoroughly enjoyed hearing the children's voices, which are central and integral to the fabric of the book.

I look forward to 'watching this space' as this wonderful book is welcomed by the early years sector throughout Scotland and beyond.

Associate Professor Sally Peters
Te Kura Toi Tangata School of Education, University of Waikato

My passion for early childhood education began as a home-based practitioner in Scotland. Later qualifying as an early childhood teacher in New Zealand, I soon became excited by research. Research interests eventually led me into the university sector, where I am now Head of the School of Education at the University of Waikato.

As a researcher, I have been fortunate to return to Scotland many times and have always been impressed by the policy and practice commitment to young children. Reflecting that commitment, the authors Michele and Avril have come together to write this informative handbook for the early years workforce. Their in-depth knowledge of what is important for children and practitioners is evident throughout the book and, while written for the early years sector in Scotland, the ideas are internationally applicable.

This delightful book invites the reader on a journey. The conversational-style text and carefully selected images can be enjoyed as a cover-to-cover read, or as a resource to dip into. Equally beneficial for the new practitioner or to inspire the experienced professional, the handbook supports all those involved in working with young children to enhance the quality of their practice. Each chapter offers clear guidelines and advice with supporting evidence about the reasons why these ideas are important. It's like a discussion with a wise friend that helps you reflect on your practice and strive to consider how children experience your setting and the impact of what you say and do. The authors' extensive understanding of children make the 'child's voice' quotations relatable and inspiring, while the adults' voices reflect what many practitioners may be thinking.

The advice aligns with research I have been involved in and highlights what is important for children's early learning. Later sections focus on practitioners embracing opportunities for professional learning, and again the authors' expertise in this area is evident in the guidance they provide.

I anticipate that readers will find this a valuable resource, a book to keep handy and return to frequently, drawing on it to answer questions, find joy in their work and be empowered to make decisions that benefit children every day. By engaging with this in-depth but accessible knowledge I am sure that readers will discover that it does, as the title indicates, have the power to transform and inspire early years practice.

Practitioner is the term used for all those working in a specific role with children in early years settings. The term also includes childminders, teachers working with young children in primary schools and those studying to achieve a practitioner qualification.

This Handbook has been designed to complement the wide range of guidance, standards and frameworks available to the early years workforce and will support the provision of high quality and meaningful experiences for our youngest children.

Introduction

How often have you heard or have been told how important your job is and how crucial your role is to the lives of our youngest children? Some people may have a perception that working with children is an easy career option when in fact you know that is far from the truth.

Passionate practitioners understand what an amazing privilege it is to work with young children and with this privilege comes a significant responsibility. Working in an early years setting can be hugely rewarding but can also be demanding and stressful. This Handbook has been designed to be both practical and accessible and aims to offer you support whilst valuing what you bring to your work with children each and every day. Feeling valued and supported in your role is vital and is as important for you as it is for children.

It is so important to acknowledge that you may also feel that you are continuously being asked to improve your practice. You are expected to be familiar with and use countless sources of information and guidance to enhance practice in relation to; child development, pedagogical approaches, working with parents, assessment, getting the learning environment right and so on.

This can cause you worry, or concern as each and every day you face challenges in getting it all right for every child and their family. This Handbook will support you to navigate through these challenges and expectations.

The Handbook is designed to help you look closely at what you really need to know, whilst discovering how to enhance and adapt your practice.

Within each chapter, through the voice of the child, there is an opportunity for you to consider what you do each day, and it will affirm for you why it is so important to 'get it right' for children. Each chapter provides clear suggestions of how to do this, which will support you in making the biggest impact in your everyday practice. The 'how you will know if you get it right for the child' in each chapter will outline observable and highly practical behaviours of a passionate practitioner.

You will no doubt remember what it was like when you began your journey in early years, when you had little or no experience and were perhaps torn between a sense of excitement and fear. It perhaps felt overwhelming (and maybe still does at times) because you believe the opinions of others matter more than your own self-belief.

Do you find yourself sometimes losing sight of why you work in early years? It is understandable if this feeling resonates with you. Keeping in mind what is really important to you in your job is key. It is important for you to enjoy the feeling of being the amazing practitioner you are. This Handbook will remind you of the importance of you!

You won't be asked to go back and 'undo' anything in your practice. You don't have to be hard on yourself for what you have not accomplished – you have only to be willing to say ''I am going to feel really good about doing my job!''

Being a professional working with young children is not simply following guidance and implementing theory, it is about your commitment to young children, your expertise and your passion. The contents of this Handbook will help to remind you why you choose to work with young children every day.

Passionate Practitioners understand the key personal skills required when working with children. It is important to take a closer look at these and at how your life experience, values and personal beliefs influence you and impact your work. There is so much to appreciate about what you bring to your role each and every day.

This is not about asking you to make huge changes to your practice, but rather to take relief from knowing that there are things that you can begin to add to or take out of your day that will make the biggest difference to the lives of children.

LET'S START
THE JOURNEY

Contents

Passionate
Practitioner

Chapter 1: Finding Your Passion
The Key to Success

Chapter 1

Being the adult children need:

"You help me to learn new things every day when you spend time with me. I need you to learn new things to build on your abilities, interests and experience. It is important for me that you find ways to develop and improve, always keeping me at the centre of your thinking".

Passion for your job is something that is felt by both you as an individual and by the children in your setting; its power should not be underestimated and that is why this is the handbook for the passionate practitioner. Passion for your role will underpin **specific knowledge, professional skills, competencies and behaviours**. This chapter will support your understanding of the skills and attributes required by practitioners; to not only evidence these positively in practice, but also to support you in recognising them in yourself.

As you work your way through this chapter consider the **specific knowledge, skills** and **attributes** needed by those working in early years. Stop, reflect, and consider what each one means to you and how you would 'measure' yourself against these, taking note of where you feel there may be opportunities for personal development.

Practitioners can sometimes feel that...

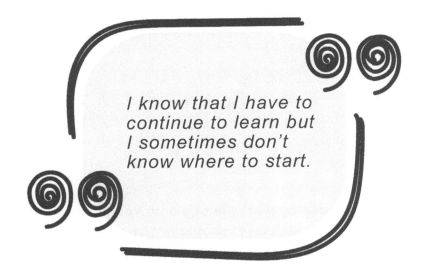

I know that I have to continue to learn but I sometimes don't know where to start.

There will be times when you have doubts about your ability to remain positive in light of the many demands on you in your everyday practice.

You may have embarked on a career in early years straight from school or you may have chosen this path as a complete change of career. Regardless, your **specific knowledge, skills** and **attributes** are pivotal to the quality of the experiences you offer young children.

Let us imagine that the children you work with could sit you down and tell you what **specific knowledge, skills** and **attributes** that they think you should have. What do you think they would say? What is it that is really important to them?

How can you be the adult they need you to be?

Children would say;

'I want to feel loved by you'

'I need to know you care'

'I need to feel that you want to be with me'

Thinking about your journey...

As a professional early years practitioner, you are required to have **specific knowledge** of theory relating to early years practice, and key in this is having an understanding of child development and what an early childhood curriculum means.

This can be considered in relation to your professional responsibilities and commitment to continuous professional learning, and when you really begin to engage in professional learning and know how vital it is in your role.

Your experience of professional learning opportunities can vary, and some will fascinate and motivate you and some you will really struggle to connect with.

We hope that as you engage with this Handbook you will find inspiration to support you as you commit to continuous professional learning.

Deciding which professional learning opportunities you should access can be challenging, but keeping up to date and ensuring you are aware of local and national guidance and relevant legislation is essential for your role.

How do you identify your professional learning needs? Do you feel confident to share that you need support to increase your knowledge in a particular area?

Knowing what your professional needs are can support your levels of confidence. As with children, it is difficult to teach an adult to be confident. The secret is to build knowledge of a situation or a subject and this will increase feelings of self-belief and competence. This will develop your confidence, which in turn will support you to observe, plan and evaluate effectively.

Being able to put into words what you actually need to support your practice may take time, but it will be worth it and will help tell the story of you and the practitioner you want to be.

Having the confidence and understanding to implement high quality learning opportunities is necessary to support children's learning and development and ideas and suggestions of how you can do this are explored throughout this Handbook.

Building and developing **specific knowledge** is hugely important and so too is having a key awareness of the professional skills and attributes required to be a passionate practitioner; the practitioner that children need you to be.

You will find many 'lists' of skills and attributes required for those working with children, and these will be evident in the person specifications of job roles. It is difficult to say if there is a 'most important' skill or attribute as so many are essential.

A child may feel it is patience and an adult may say it is communication. Undoubtedly everyone benefits when both are in abundance.

Your skills of communication

Communication is key in all aspects of our lives, and it is important to remember that non-verbal communication is recognised to be more powerful than verbal communication, for example your facial expressions. Developing and reflecting on all of these will support your practice with both children and adults. We must all remember the power of a smile, a look of encouragement, of wonder, warmth and affection.

Communication skills are integral to your skills of observation. As you engage with children, being an active listener will support you in adopting a rich questioning approach, having a significant influence on children's experiences. Your observation skills are vital and will inform how you plan and assess children's learning. As you observe you see possibilities for individual children, and your observations allow you to consider the 'what if' for children. It may be *'what if I give that look of encouragement, a child will progress in their learning'* or *'what if I provide a word, a resource; will it take them further in their learning journey?'*

Your skills of observation and communication enable endless possibilities. Read on to discover more about this.

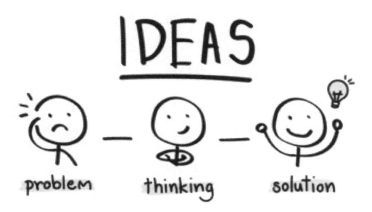

Your skills of creativity

You may think that means you have to be artistic, be the person who creates interesting displays around the early years setting. Yes, it is important that you are inspired and confident to make the environment interesting and inviting but it is also important that you are the person who inspires problem solving, who nurtures curiosity, who feeds the imagination, and be the person who role models open-mindedness. These skills are vital in the provision of high quality environments.

Your professional qualities and behaviours

Do you spark joy for the children in your care? Do the other adults in your workplace feel the joy you have for your job? Joy, like confidence, can be difficult to 'learn' but it would be difficult not to assume that as you build confidence in your practice, it can be observed as joy. You may not feel comfortable describing yourself as someone who is joyful, yet you may be described as an adult who displays happiness and pleasure. To a child this can be observed as joy, and that can be infectious.

Often skills and qualities are inter-related – take patience for example; are you naturally patient, or is it something you can learn? What is a child's measure of patience, and would they describe you as patient?

It is so important that a child feels a sense of patience in your presence. Consider the many learning experiences a child can engage in whilst in an early years setting. As you reflect on this you will undoubtedly have numerous examples and as you know, learning takes place in diverse ways, and having and feeling the reassurance of others around you can have a hugely positive effect.

Building attachments with children relies on genuine interest and a willingness to connect. The quality of these attachments is enriched when connections are felt and developed by both parties. Just as a child needs to feel the genuine interest of an adult, the quality of the relationship is enhanced when children feel genuine interest towards the adult.

You are a significant role-model to children and your positive attitude will influence children as they develop their own skills and attributes.

What skills and qualities are you drawn to in other people? Do you connect with someone who displays empathy? Do you enjoy being in the company of someone who is compassionate and sensitive to your needs and feelings?

As an adult, the sense of security that you feel when someone shows an understanding of your thoughts and feelings can be powerful, and this is also felt significantly by young children.

Children are not only sensitive but also intuitive and they seek the genuine care and attention of the adults looking after them. It is important to understand what empathy look likes from the eyes of a child. The quality of the relationship between an adult and a child relies upon the depth of understanding between both parties and empathy relies on a commitment and appreciation of the feelings of others.

Children will look to you for inspiration, and this might be when they are trying something new or are faced with a challenge. Regardless of the situation this inspiration will rely on your levels of enthusiasm, your energy, your confidence, and your knowledge.

Children will not remember you for the material things you provided, but for the feeling that you cherished them.

~Richard L. Evans

www.SpirituallyThinking.blogspot.com

Your knowledge of child development

Are you intrigued by the ways children develop? Having a genuine interest in child development is core to the provision of high quality learning experiences and your ability to seek to understand where individual children are in their development is essential. When this genuine interest is coupled with other skills and attributes, such as having a flexible approach and knowledge of how young children learn, you will feel your confidence grow as you will see children respond positively to the experiences and engagement you provide.

Connecting with the feelings and thoughts of young children will build compassion that is felt by them. Do you feel equipped to explore this? It is important to think of the many attributes you have that will support the quality of your connections. It is hoped that the chapters within this Handbook will build on your existing knowledge and attributes.

It is also hoped that this Handbook will enthuse you and give you confidence for those times when children 'need' you to inspire them. You won't always have the answers but if you are committed to your role then the answers will come. Remember that children are very forgiving, and they will welcome your honesty, but they also need you to believe in both them and you whilst ensuring your enthusiasm is tangible.

At the start of this chapter the focus on the need for you to have specific knowledge, skills and attributes is clear. Take some time to consider how these have been outlined throughout this chapter. You will find a *Scale for Reflection* at the back of the Handbook to support your reflective journey. Try to be honest and reflect on where you feel you would like to focus personally. Always consider the results that children would 'give to you'.

Children can potentially be our fiercest critics, but they are so very deserving of our honest reflection and our commitment to be our very best self for them.

Remember, enthusiasm and motivation can be infectious and as you now work your way through the Handbook, think how knowing yourself better will support you to engage with the many practical suggestions you will see.

Small things that you can do that will make the biggest difference:

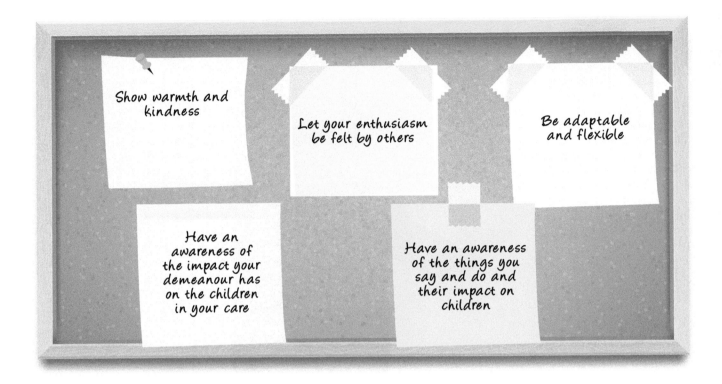

Show warmth and kindness

Let your enthusiasm be felt by others

Be adaptable and flexible

Have an awareness of the impact your demeanour has on the children in your care

Have an awareness of the things you say and do and their impact on children

You will know when you have built upon your abilities, interests and experience when the children around you...

know you are really listening to them

look into your eyes and see your enthusiasm

see themselves as unique and important

know they can come to you and be met with care and understanding

know you will be patient with them

see you are passionate about what you do

Being a Passionate Practitioner – Your Journey

Scale for Reflection

At the back of this Handbook you will find a Scale for Reflection. This tool will help you to measure where you are and support you to focus on identified areas of your practice.

Ongoing self-reflection makes you better equipped to take a balanced view of your practice, recognising what works well and identifying the things that you do that have a positive impact.

It's not about focusing on where you're going wrong, but about seeing it as a positive and gratifying process. It shows where you are on your journey, acknowledging what you have done and celebrating your successes.

Self-reflection is also about asking yourself some important questions; not only about what you do in your daily practice, but also why you choose to do those things the way you do, what has led you to the approaches you take and how your actions have impacted on children.

Reflective practice is about helping us improve but it doesn't always mean having to change what we are already doing. It's about gathering information to help us make the right decisions.

Passionate
Practitioner

Chapter 2: Delighting in Your Work
Bringing the Joy

Chapter 2

"I want you to find out what brings me joy and to help me to learn new things"

When asked, "What is it about your work that you really enjoy and like the most?", practitioners often respond with a sentiment that goes something like, "I just love being with the children..." "It's the joy I get each day as I work with young children and their families."

Working with children is a multi-layered, complex, and dynamic role and is fundamentally about relationships, about love, about caring, and let's not forget, about joy and fun.

Practitioners often say when talking about children's experiences;

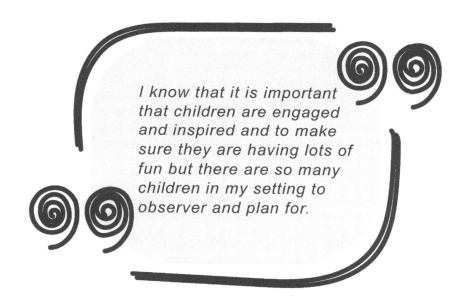

I know that it is important that children are engaged and inspired and to make sure they are having lots of fun but there are so many children in my setting to observer and plan for.

It is important to acknowledge that what you are asked to do can sometimes make you feel a little overwhelmed. Do you feel a bit unsure, and perhaps question if you are able to do what is being asked of you?

We sometimes forget that a child's world is fresh, new and beautiful, it is full of wonder and excitement.

Bringing to mind those amazing feelings...

Taking some time to remember great times, wonderful experiences and special moments; things that really delighted you, is a good place to start and will support you with feeling uncertain.

Think of something right now that really gives or has given you a **sense of wonder**.

These feelings of wonder make us aware that we have experienced something special and gives us an appreciation of the world.

Curiosity and wonder are so evident in the enthusiasm of young children and these expressions of their interest are so much a part of their charm.

Finding the joy

In your setting, children come with many different interests and a variety of learning styles. The key for you, is to try to look out for what really fascinates and inspires each and every child. Don't be in a rush about this and try to remember it may only become clear that a child has certain preferences and interests after getting to know them over a period of time.

As you slowly get to know each child's preferences; maybe it's the sand or water play that makes them happy, perhaps role play or being outdoors, you start to learn what really makes their eyes light up with delight and eagerness.

When we see happy children, it really can make us happy too and it is important that you share in their joy as much as possible.

Noticing the joy

Looking around your setting, observing children at play and exploring, do you often see them full of joy and wonder? This can be evident when children are deeply engrossed in their play, when there is lots of chatter and they are full of happiness.

Observing how absorbed and engaged children are as they interact and play lets us understand what they really like to do. It is so important to include this in any of your note taking, as these positive experiences are recognised as being crucial for children's learning and development

Our enthusiastic response to children's interests is the surest way to take the next step and engage them in some form of meaningful conversation or interaction. Children can be deeply disappointed when, for whatever reason, adults do not respond with enthusiasm …and have all had that experience from time to time!

Think about the times when a child's joy has been infectious, for example, splashing in puddles, dancing in bare feet, or catching bubbles. We recognise and accept this kind of play, valuing it for what it provides for the child; a release of physical energy, a sense of power, and often an expression of pure joy.

All too often, in busy early years settings, significant moments of children's joy can be overlooked. Revisiting, reflecting on and sharing joyful moments can be rewarding and affirming - a reminder of the delight of working with children and their families.

Be guided by what inspires and captivates children's interests

It is those amazing moments that 'wow' and captivate children, that cause their eyes to shine and their tongues to stick out in deep concentration!

When we see children deeply engaged and involved with their experiences - that is when real learning happens.

Children learn things in life by observing people as they grow. They watch their parents/carers and other adults around them, noting everything they say and do. We have to be aware that children are always watching, mirroring what we do and following our examples in the way we deal with everyday situations.

Therefore, it is so important that we live our lives in accordance with our values, know who we are and the kind of individual we want to be. Much of our life is spent in the company of young children and we will influence the older child, adolescent and adult they will become.

When children have positive role models to follow, they have the potential to become responsible, caring, considerate adults.

Pause for thought...

When we forget to pause and take a breath, we miss the opportunity to connect with ourselves and be truly in the present.

As practitioners, when we can do this a little more, we can make better choices for ourselves and for children. Learning to delight a little more in what you do and savouring the moments that you spend with a child, will help you better understand what they need from you.

Research shows that happy and content people give themselves ongoing reassurance, acknowledgment, praise and even pep talks. This can seem strange at first, but why not try to talk to yourself out loud, so children can hear you...

"I know that I am good at so many things."

"It's ok if I make mistakes sometimes."

"I don't have to get everything done right now."

"I'm getting better at doing this every time I try!"

We all need to have a sense of joy and wonder in order to be able to recognise and value it in children. Keep in mind that adults and children have different ways of thinking about time, so it's important for us to understand that children are often more focused on immediate happiness, whereas adults often tend to focus on a child's future happiness.

Why not focus upon how you can add more joy, wonder and imagination into the activities and experiences you offer.

Bear in mind that you won't be able to do this all the time but when you do, you can nudge or drive a child's play into deep involvement. The reward will be when the child becomes empowered to discover more, to explore, to wallow in the fun of it.

Try to find ways to make changes so that children can be more relaxed and comfortable in the spaces you create for them.

The joy of helping children to learn new things

Children, like all of us, like to have some control of their own learning and choices. Let them be in the driver's seat! A really good way to do this is to try to provide plenty of options and choices, which is a great way to connect with them too.

If you really want to help children to learn, then the key is to find things for them to be curious about and things that fascinate them. Enthusiasm is powerful, especially when it comes to learning new things.

"Let me explore, try new things, make mistakes, discover, so that I can be independent and become more confident."

It is tricky at times, to know if a child has learned something new. Begin by reflecting on what you have seen the child enjoy doing and try to work out what they are trying to understand.

You may find some of these questions helpful when reflecting on your observations of play;

- *How interested was the child in what they were doing? Were they deeply involved in their play? Did they seem intent on what they were doing or did they seem more interested in what others were doing?*

- *What was the child's approach to the materials or activity? Was the child slow in getting started or did they dive right in?*

- *What do you think the child already knew about these materials or the activity?*

- *Did you notice something new? Did they use materials or explore spaces in a variety of ways?*

- *How do you think the child felt about what they were doing? Did they seem happy, engaged or satisfied? Did they ask for help or seem to need some encouragement?*

- *What kinds of changes were there between the beginning and the end of the activity? Did the child's behaviour change as they played?*

Listening and watching is a crucial part of gaining access to children's ideas and feelings. However, we must be aware of seeing what is truly happening as opposed to what we want to see. It is helpful for practitioners to look more closely at the actual play experiences of children, to notice the subtleties of what children are doing and saying.

Try to model a sense of amazement for even the smallest wonders. Comment out loud to children about the astonishing things you see, hear and feel every day.

Take the opportunity, when you can, to discover new things and learn together. As a child sees the joy and excitement that this brings to you; they'll begin to share your enthusiasm and the joy of learning new things.

Small things that you can do that will make the biggest difference:

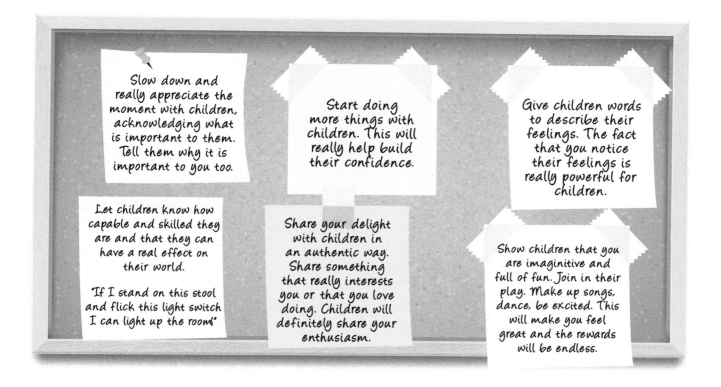

You will know what brings me joy and helps me to learn new things when I...

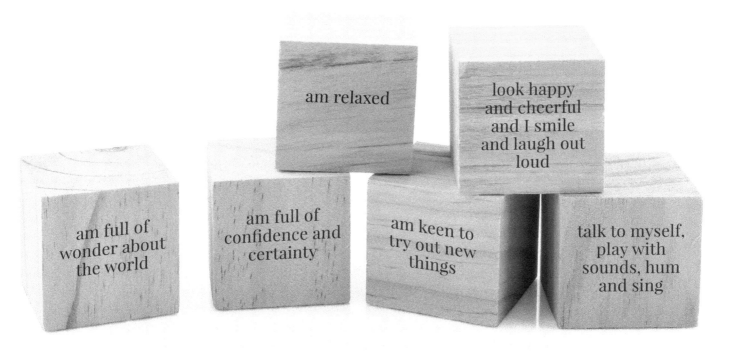

Chapter 3: The Power of Your Sense of Humour

Chapter 3

"It's hard sometimes but I would love you to smile more, and for us to laugh together more."

You might be thinking as you read this that it won't be possible to try to smile all day, but it is not about having to try to smile, it is about having that inner sense of confidence and joy that makes smiling instinctive and involuntary. Smiling can be a superpower!

The importance of building meaningful relationships in early years settings cannot be undervalued and these positive relationships can grow through high quality connections. However, if we acknowledge that babies and children are instinctively social beings, then how you connect with young children is hugely important and so too is the quality of these connections.

You might be thinking that you are unsure what high quality connections are or what they might 'look' like.

The important thing to remember is that they don't have to be learned and they can also be very subtle. When children know that you have noticed them or are interested in them, then connections become high quality.

Practitioners may wonder;

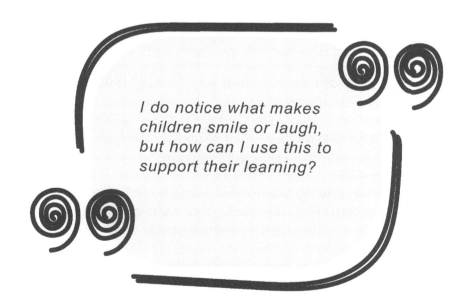

I do notice what makes children smile or laugh, but how can I use this to support their learning?

Children thrive on continuity, and your responses to children can be fundamental in supporting this. Do children feel assured that you will be the person whose eyes sparkle with delight when they arrive in the setting, when they share a thought, an idea, an achievement? Do children know that when any of this is happening in their world, you will be the person who will reward them with a smile, or with laughter?

Sharing happy experiences are an excellent way to build high quality connections with children, and indeed with adults.

'I love it when we laugh together. It makes me feel so good and, when you do, I love being around you'

Laughing is recognised as having positive effects on mental health. Science tells us that laughter releases endorphins, the 'feel good' natural chemicals, it can reduce stress and importantly, can build and strengthen social connections.

When we think about all the benefits, it can be hard to think of a reason why we wouldn't want to share laughter with children, and have fun.

If you acknowledge the power that laughter has in building strong connections; when you wholeheartedly accept its power, it can lead to a realisation of the benefits for mental and emotional health.

As you embrace your role as a passionate practitioner you are acutely aware of the need to create attachments and strong bonds with children and laughter can support this. Most importantly, it has benefits for everyone invested in creating strong bonds through meaningful connections.

Coming to an early years setting can be a stressful situation for some children, and for some parents too. They may arrive experiencing a sense of anxiousness or worry, or sometimes sadness. It is at these times, the power of your smile, your warmth and compassion can come to the fore. This 'tool' from your 'toolbox' can have a significant impact on diffusing these feelings, with the knowledge too that you are building those high quality connections.

Think of the times where you have engaged in a game of 'peek a boo' with a baby or young child. This may have been within your setting, or even on a bus or a train, but the memory you will have, is hopefully one of joy and laughter; the sound of a child's laughter resonating in your mind, making you smile. In that moment you were building connections, you were supporting the release of endorphins for you and that child, and you were laying foundations for good mental health.

Are you committed to creating high quality connections with the children you work with?

Think of the feelings you experience when someone smiles at you, especially when they smile with their eyes. A smile is hugely powerful and cannot be underestimated. The amazing thing about a smile is that it not only makes the person on the receiving end feel good, it can make the person offering the smile feel good too.

As children and families enter your setting, they bring a range of emotions with them. Regardless of the feelings and emotions they are experiencing, they need to be welcomed with a smile to create a sense of security. The facial expressions of those welcoming children and families can have a significant impact on their levels of confidence.

The feelings children experience when they are in your care can have a significant effect on their ability to deal with emotions and sometimes these emotions can be intense; they may be sad, worried or angry. Your reactions and interactions with children can relax them and support them to see things in a different way, equipping them to deal with their emotions.

Laughter is said to increase our stress resilience, which is an amazing gift that you can give our youngest children.

'I am so grateful that you take time to have fun with me and I know it must be hard when there are so many other children and so much to do'

Fun and laughter are amazing tools, particularly when you consider the huge benefits.

Do you think that children look at you and feel that sense of fun, are you the person that makes them smile and give them that lovely, joyful feeling - even when they bring you a worm?

It is recognised that around 80% of what we are feeling is communicated through our body language. When you consider this, it will hopefully make you reflect on how connections can be significantly influenced through those shared experiences that do not involve language. This is where those smiles, the laughter, the meaningful eye contact can be so very important.

Sometimes you might be feeling less positive or not so 'full of joy'; not able to tune into the feelings that children are experiencing but try to reflect on the power a child's smile or laughter can have to make you feel better. Sharing these high quality connections can benefit all involved.

Children are highly skilled at tuning in and they can do this through observation of an adult's facial expressions. Children love to see your face as you bring a story to life, the grumpy bear, the curious kitten. Opportunities such as this offer endless opportunities for fun! Think of a time when someone has told you a funny story; what made you laugh? Was it the story itself or the joy and laughter the 'story teller' brought to the story? Regardless of the answer, the end result for all involved would have been the release of those endorphins and the connections with the 'story teller'.

Humour and laughter are so much more than just a means to entertain, they provide an opportunity to process information, make sense of a situation, be it through words or expressions, or indeed sounds. They have the power to create a sense of pleasure and can create a positive atmosphere.

A positive atmosphere in your setting is really important, and you have a key role to play in that. Usually in an early years setting, there are many differing personalities and for some, telling a funny story about a situation will be easier than it is for others but do not fear if you wouldn't describe yourself as naturally boisterous or outgoing.

Laughter and fun can be nurtured from the smallest most intimate situation and the laughter does not have to be loud or raucous, it merely has to be felt and given an opportunity to be expressed. Creating those opportunities can be so powerful for you as a practitioner and when you feel the influence of that power on the connections you have with the children in your setting, you will strive to create more opportunities, shared experiences, and fundamentally, high quality connections.

'Let's laugh together as much as we can'

'A good time to laugh is anytime you can'

- Linda Ellerbee

Small things that you can do that will make the biggest difference:

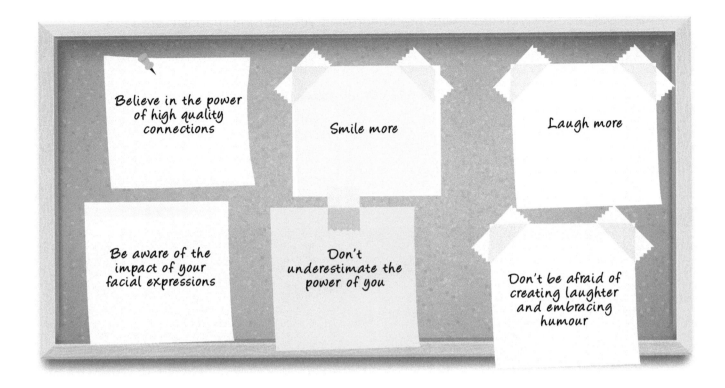

You will know what brings me joy and helps me to learn new things when...

50

Passionate
Practitioner

Chapter 4: The Art of Listening

Chapter 4

"I know it takes up your time, but I want you to care about what I think and, say and really give me time to talk."

When asked, "What are the challenges of finding time to talk with children during your day?" practitioners often respond with sentiments that go something like,

"I feel like the day always runs away from me".

'"I have to juggle too many tasks" or

"I'm always being interrupted!"

In our fast-paced daily lives, when we are trying to keep up with everything coming at us that we need to give our attention to, focusing on others, listening to what they have to say, and giving our full attention for significant periods of time, can feel overwhelming and can take substantial emotional strength.

The best gift you can give to another person is staying focused upon them, making a real effort to understand what they are trying to communicate and listening to every word.

Listening is a skill. It takes a bit of practice to get better at it but it also has the effect of making you become a much better communicator and a person that other people want to be around. Honing in on those listening skills is extremely valuable.

If you don't think this is a strong trait of yours, try taking a few of these steps to see if you can strengthen your listening power;

Deliver your questions with true curiosity and a desire to learn more. Develop a few good open ended questions and practice them.

Try hard not to cut children off before they have finished speaking. It's easy to form an opinion or reject children's views before they finish what they have to say.

See how long you can go in coversation by sharing little and listening a bit more.

We all think faster than we speak. Children often take longer than adults to find the right word. Listening patiently, as though you have lots of time, is really hard in your busy day but it's good for you to pause for a moment or two to do this.

Keep in mind that many messages children send us can be communicated without words for example through tone of voice, posture, energy level, facial expression or change in behaviour.

Practitioners may say, when talking about conversations with children;

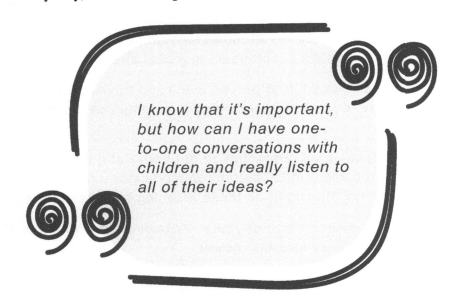

I know that it's important, but how can I have one-to-one conversations with children and really listen to all of their ideas?

It is recognised that early years practitioners are characterised by their commitment to children – their enthusiasm, enjoyment and interest in their work and their ability to 'tune' into children.

It is so important to acknowledge how **each and every day** you respond sensitively to the moment-on-moment changing emotions, needs and wishes of the children in your setting.

Just for a moment recognise just how much you value the children you work with. You value them for who they are, what they know and understand, their experiences, their skills and all the important aspects of their lives that you become familiar with as you turn your attention to them and truly see and hear them.

"I feel happy and secure wherever I am, knowing you are there for me when I need you."

It is good to acknowledge that our world revolves around our thoughts; what we know and feel about things, what we care about, and whether other people care about us.

Being listened to and heard is one of our greatest desires and we definitely know what it's like when we don't feel listened to.

Think about a time when someone brushed off what you were trying to say and made you feel unimportant.

We all need to feel that what we have to say matters.

One of the very best things we can do with young children is to have interesting and enjoyable conversations with them.

There can be a temptation to treat conversations with children differently from adult conversations, as though they perhaps should be more simplistic.

Do you have set ideas about what children are likely to say, do you pretend you always know what to do or sometimes not to listen at all because you lack confidence or are worried that you will get it 'wrong'?

As part of our day, we can all spend a bit too much time issuing commands: "we have to do this now", "time to listen," "quiet everyone!".

Try to keep in mind what it is that you love about hearing what children have to say; from being involved in hearing about experiences that delight them or enjoying times where you have a warm, calm and comforting chat.

The key to valuing what a child has to say, is to join in sensitively with any type of play, whether it be physical games like chase, doing puzzles together, or sensory play such as playing in the sand.

Research makes a good case for giving pretend play special status when it comes to encouraging young children to communicate with you. Have fun finding your inner child and using your imagination with children!

We are often asked to be responsive and to ensure that children are making sustained progress in their learning. – what does this really mean?

Being More Responsive to Children Really means:

Thinking together to help children make sense of experiences

Learning from and exploring alongside children to find things out rather than providing immediate answers

Encouraging children to think more deeply and 'tease out' their ideas

Following the child's lead to find what is really important and interesting to them

Listening to children by mirroring their play or repeating back what they say

Valuing children's decisions and choices and asking them to explain them to you

As a result of us being more responsive, children will start to trust us and be more likely to feel secure within themselves.

If we only want to have a conversation to get a correct answer, or the best solution, then we really are missing the point. That won't leave any room for you both to wrestle with new ideas and concepts - where the real learning takes place.

This can actually be a lot of fun – especially when you commit to thinking of fun and playful things to do together.

The brilliant thing is that you will begin to notice that your responsiveness has revealed more to you about the child.

What you will also notice are the ways that your relationships with children will have changed and grown.

We all know how important it is to receive undivided attention when you are sharing your thoughts. This is something that children really do need but if you can't listen at a particular moment, that's alright, just explain why and assure them that you will listen to what they have to say shortly.

Really hearing what a child has to say

Recognising the critical importance of children communicating with us, is the best place to start. Acknowledging that relationships between practitioners and children are greatly improved when there is good communication taking place is key.

Are you a good communicator?

Most of us also know that sometimes communicating with others can be a difficult and often disappointing experience. There are times when we mean well, but the way we say things can be misunderstood.

An important step in developing communication skills, for ourselves and for children, is to be open to talking about all kinds of feelings, including anger, joy, frustration, fear and anxiety. In children this really helps develop a 'feelings' vocabulary.

Take opportunities to prompt children to tell you how they feel by describing what you think they're feeling – for example, 'It sounds like you felt left out when Nathan wanted to play with those children'. Ask the child to help you understand.

What we all know about early years settings is that they can be distracting places, so how can practitioners find the time and focus to talk in depth with children?

One of the biggest challenges for practitioners in early years settings, is finding time and space to have the types of deep conversations that children really want and need.

Being the kind of communicator, where you and the child can share ideas that extend their understanding further is a huge priority. That said, do you often find yourself using what could be called 'organising language', where most of what you say involves managing children and encouraging them to behave 'appropriately'?

We can be so 'on the go' that we are only able to pay fleeting attention to what children are saying. Every single practitioner feels like that at some points during a busy session. A passionate practitioner will be aware of this and grow in their reflections of these situations.

The message we want to communicate to children is, "Take your time. I'm not going anywhere." This is preferred, but often adult-to-child ratios, in particular, may not allow for this.

However, you can plan for this to happen during the times that children are going to benefit most from in-depth conversation, for example, during outdoor play or during a story. Plan to 'plant yourself' at activities that the child has initiated.

- Make some suggestions

- Remind children that you are listening

- Emphasise that what they say is important to you;
  "That's interesting."   "Explain that to me."

- Repeating or rephrasing what the child has said from time to time, lets them know you're listening and helps you check what they are really saying.

Why not ask children to help take photographs of what they have been doing? You can then share the photos with the children the next day. Maybe write down their comments with them, celebrating what you have been doing together and display the comments and photos together.

Keep in mind...

Children will have differing experiences of the types of interactions they have with the adults in their lives. Some may not have the opportunity to have significant amounts of quality time talking with an adult at all.

Try not to make structured observations during those focused conversations and interactions. It's best for you both that you're not taking notes while playing and talking together as the child senses that you are not completely focusing on the conversation, and that lovely closeness that you have created can disappear.

We know that one of the most important considerations for practitioners in all early years settings is to treat children with respect and value their opinions.

We are told;

"All children should feel as though they have a voice and feel safe to express that voice"

Does this make you pause for thought?

Hearing children's voices can tell us what is important to them. **Is hearing what children have to say really that important to you?**

Think about the last time you tried to have a genuinely meaningful conversation with a child. How successful were you?

Sometimes we do this before we have built up enough knowledge of the child. This really does take a bit of time so always factor that in.

Having quality conversations with children is **highly skilled work** so whenever you can, try to slow down, take stock and really focus on getting to know the child a little better. Then you can look for evidence of the choices that they make and how their behaviour changes through that interaction with you.

How much value should we place on incorporating and taking account of children's voices?

Values can conflict with one another

If for example, you value both listening to children but also think that they shouldn't be too over-confident and outspoken... a question to ask is..."what do I consider important, and which of these values is more important to me?".

It's best to take a bit of time to clarify what your own values and beliefs are and decide how effective you think children really are in sharing their thoughts and ideas, especially when you are being asked to involve children in planning their learning experiences.

Many questions and uncertainties arise as practitioners consider the best way to involve children in planning their learning. Having this expectation can feel like this is just another addition to the paperwork pile.

It can be really daunting knowing that you need to spend quite a bit of time with each child to build trust, understanding and positive relationships. But try to always keep in mind that this can also be hugely rewarding and enjoyable.

Small things that you can do that will make the biggest difference:

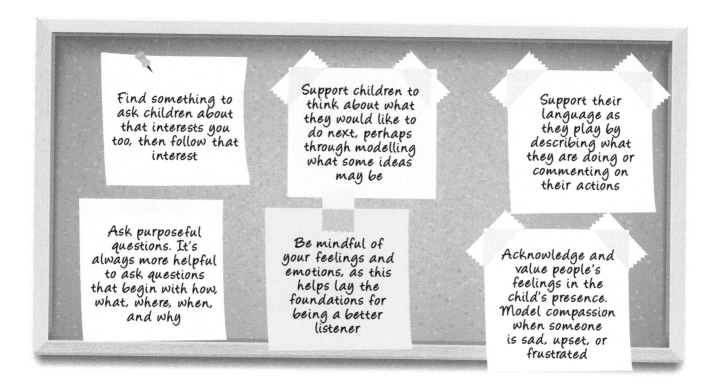

Find something to ask children about that interests you too, then follow that interest

Support children to think about what they would like to do next, perhaps through modelling what some ideas may be

Support their language as they play by describing what they are doing or commenting on their actions

Ask purposeful questions. It's always more helpful to ask questions that begin with how, what, where, when, and why

Be mindful of your feelings and emotions, as this helps lay the foundations for being a better listener

Acknowledge and value people's feelings in the child's presence. Model compassion when someone is sad, upset, or frustrated

You will know when I feel you care about what I think and say and really give me time to talk when...

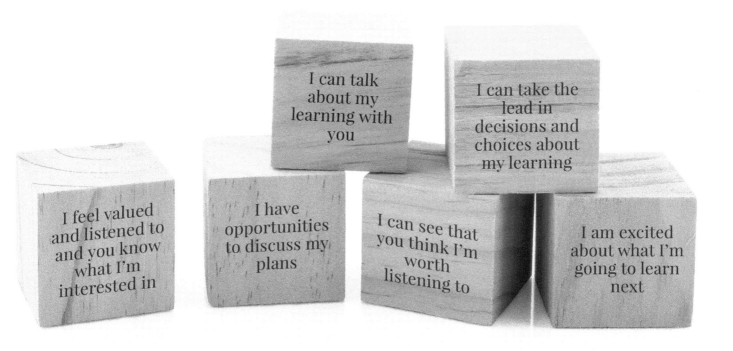

I can talk about my learning with you

I can take the lead in decisions and choices about my learning

I feel valued and listened to and you know what I'm interested in

I have opportunities to discuss my plans

I can see that you think I'm worth listening to

I am excited about what I'm going to learn next

Passionate
Practitioner

Chapter 5: Enticing and Enriching Play Spaces

Chapter 5

"I want you to create an environment for me to learn best, in a place which is inviting, stimulating challenging and empowering."

Let's imagine, that as you enter a busy playroom or play space, lots of children come flocking around you, eager to engage with you and seeming to prefer being with you than doing anything else.

It could be that they really love your company and are eager to spend time with you. Perhaps they enjoy conversations with you and know that you will listen to them.

But it's always useful to wonder; are they coming to spend time with me because they can't find anything else they'd like to do? Do I have too little available to stimulate these children? Am I really just their main point of interest?

We all understand how important it is to provide each child with a place where they are **acknowledged, challenged and empowered**.

An environment lacking stimulation and challenge can result in children appearing a little bored and flitting from one activity to the next or looking for adults to talk to or to help find them something to do.

The first thing to try if this happens, is to help the child on their way by offering comments or suggestions such as: "What a good idea you just had!" "What do you think you will need to make that cave you were talking about?" "If we go over there, what do you think we could do?

Practitioners may say;

How can I possibly create challenging and stimulating experiences for every child in my setting?

Where do you start...?

...by focusing upon and acknowledging that any learning spaces you create **need to reflect the children you have right now in your setting**.

As soon as a child becomes part of an early years setting, passionate practitioners will do everything they can to really get to know them. They find out so much about them each day, just by their interactions and the connections they make with them. That is significant and will make a huge difference for all involved.

"Take time to watch me play so that you can see what I like to do and try to talk to me as often as you can."

Looking at your play spaces with FRESH EYES

A good way to gauge how stimulating and engaging your spaces are is to see the environment through the eyes of the child.

Then ask yourself these questions;

• What are the play experiences really like for children?

• What are children experiencing during play?

• What does the play experience mean for the child?

• What kind of things are the children actually learning about as a result of these experiences?

Through their eyes...

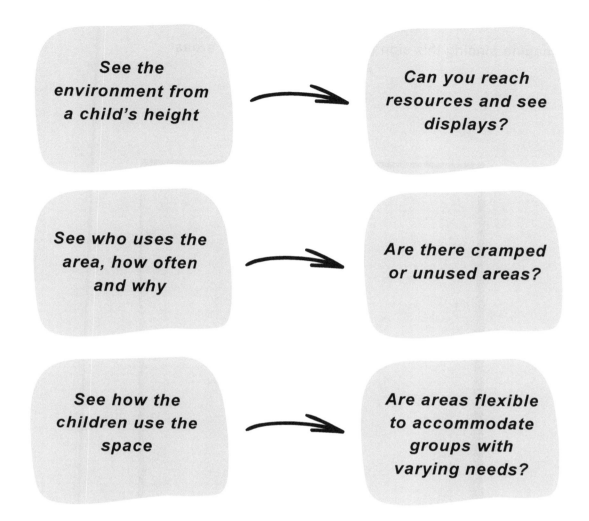

See the environment from a child's height	→	Can you reach resources and see displays?
See who uses the area, how often and why	→	Are there cramped or unused areas?
See how the children use the space	→	Are areas flexible to accommodate groups with varying needs?

Starting from a child's perspective

Do we know what each child really **loves** to do?

The way the environment is designed and organised, influences how children feel, act, and behave.

The trick is to focus on children's needs before you start designing and developing any play space.

Think about how excited children get when you have, for example, changed the home area or play materials – everyone wants to get in there to play! You know that sometimes just displaying objects in different ways can spark their curiosity.

We all want children to be busy and purposeful but before you reach for a box of toys, equipment or construction materials; something to fill a tuff tray or a play space, just pause.

Take a little time to think of ways for children to be presented with materials in new and interesting ways. In young children, curiosity is largely spontaneous, as they are attracted to new and interesting things.

Then imagine pinning this sign up in one of your play areas!

Sometimes we can disconnect ourselves from children's play spaces. The challenge for us all, is to get a bit more involved and really question when we overlook children who are 'busy playing' as we can miss so much and the genuine value of what a child is actually doing, can be missed.

Really notice children at play

Listen to their conversations.

Think about the questions they are asking.

Think about what you have heard.

Then you can decide what that means for you.

Does it mean re-thinking what is being offered to children, adding or removing materials or finding new ways to grab children's interest and to spark their curiosity?

Children want us to provide things that they will find fascinating, so why not try positioning some materials 'out of place'; things with which children may not be familiar in a particular space, prompting them to ask questions. Think of these as invitations to play.

It may be useful to think of these invitations a bit more specifically, such as an invitation to count, an invitation to play imaginatively or an invitation to build.

Theory and philosophy, acknowledge the real progress children make in their learning when the adult and child work together

Children do not touch, see, or hear passively; they feel, look, and listen actively.

Children express their curiosity through all of their senses: 'What does it look like or feel like?' 'What does it sound, smell or taste like?'

It is good to notice in your setting, the kinds of things you offer to children to stimulate their senses and help them to generate ideas.

It is useful to think about the use of 'authentic' resources. These are simple real-life items that children may have experienced before. These items can become opportunities for intrigue, play and curiosity.

Focus on asking; "What do I want the environment to look and feel like for children?"

Imagine it the way you want it to be

When you turn your focus to one particular aspect of a child's play, such as how purposeful they are or how absorbed they are in what they are doing, then over time, you can discover what new learning has emerged.

Through offering opportunities for children to explore, to be curious and to find things that interest them, you can begin to build a picture of the child as a thinker and a learner.

Most importantly, your positive state of mind; full of enthusiasm, love and interest can be a child's motivation to be inspired and to learn new things.

A fundamental question to ask ourselves about any provision, material, space or display in our learning environment...

What is it for?

Once you can put in to words **why** you have it and **who** you have it for, acknowledging and supporting children's personal or group interests, planning then becomes a much simpler task.

Challenge Through Enriching Play Spaces

Studies in neuroscience tell us that a frequent change of materials, experiences, and environment provides novelty for the brain. Attention is drawn to things that are unusual or new.

Rather than change the whole environment, we can create a range of spaces where children feel confident to tackle new challenges, and where they can make mistakes and see this as part of the learning process.

It is important to note that in challenging children, we are not escalating learning - we are enriching it. For example, when a child learns a skill, such as being able to coordinate their small fingers and carefully manipulate beads onto a string, we don't automatically move to asking them to sew with a needle and thread. Instead, we challenge them to use and hone these fine, finger movement skills across a range of activities and practical everyday tasks.

Since children need to maintain focus for learning to take place, you only need to take a familiar activity or a newly acquired skill and apply it to new situations or materials.

We are then also questioning ourselves, by reflecting on the ways we provide problems to solve and challenges for children within play.

Can you build a stable big enough for two horses?

Can you try to make the shadows look like people?

Small things that you can do that will make the biggest difference:

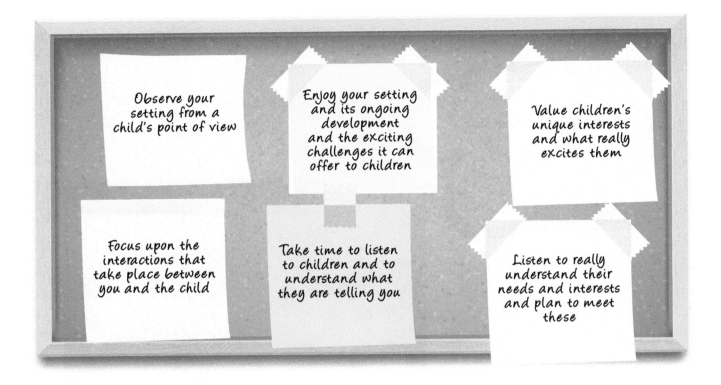

You will know when you have created an environment for me which is inviting, stimulating challenging and empowering when you...

Chapter 6: The Magic of Creativity and Self Expression

Chapter 6

"I really want you to think of ways to encourage me to express myself; to discover things, create things, invent things and use my imagination."

You may recognise the situation where you observe a child deeply involved in their play with a range of coloured pens. Instinctively, you try to be encouraging and ask them, "What are you making?" and they shrug. Until you mentioned it, they hadn't given it any thought. It is worth considering why you asked the question in the first place.

It can be tricky to avoid asking children to put a "label" on their artwork. It's likely that they are exploring materials and how they relate to each other as opposed to communicating an idea through what they have made.

As we know, young children love the way it feels when they smear paint across paper, how it looks when they add a touch of glitter, and even the soft sound a paint brush makes.

If a child were to present their 'creation' to you and say "Look what I made!", what do you usually say to them?

Most of the time, if a child shows what they have created to an adult, they will say one of three things:

1.   It's beautiful!

2.   I love it!

3.   What is it?

We know how important it is to nurture children's creativity early on in their development. So how can we let children know that we value their work?

The best way to do this is by not making assumptions about it.

Young children are proud of their creations. They enjoy the process and are usually satisfied with the results.

Once they have completed their creative activity, listen carefully to anything they might want to say about it. Try not to push or pry; just pause and listen. Look for what they might be trying to communicate. Ask a few questions, and listen for the answers. Don't be tempted to interpret what the child has produced.

You can find something specific and authentic to comment on.

"I like how you decided to change your mind and use that box on your model instead – it really works!"

"Yes, I noticed that you added lots of buildings/trees/people, etc. into your drawing."

Some practitioners say, when talking about creative experiences for children;

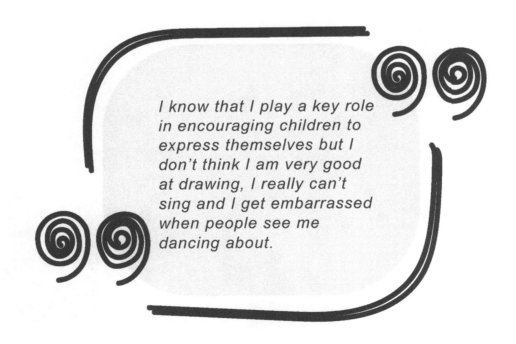

I know that I play a key role in encouraging children to express themselves but I don't think I am very good at drawing, I really can't sing and I get embarrassed when people see me dancing about.

Just as you don't judge children in their expressions of art or singing and dancing, or indeed those of your colleagues, do your best not to judge yourself.

Do you lack confidence in your ability to promote creativity and creative learning? Some practitioners may think that they do not have any creative ability or expertise – this might resonate with you.

It is important that we, as adults working with children, feel at ease with our own creative abilities.

The good news is that you don't have to be a talented artist or singer or indeed have any particular creative talents.

'I'd like you to set up places where I can play and express myself and where I can join in with others when I want to, and I love it when you join in too'

Some practitioners feel so uncomfortable with the idea of promoting activities that encourage self-expression that they might avoid them or may use quite structured approaches to children's creative learning experiences.

How often do our own anxieties lead to providing creative activities that are perhaps a little limited in scope, or letting other people take the lead without really acknowledging our own inhibitions?

You may have to switch your thinking about the activity, and it may be that you could find a way to, for example:

- acknowledge that we don't teach children to be creative by demonstrating our artistic skills.

- allow for a little more 'messiness' and experimenting. A creative process can be unpredictable, so it is helpful to try to be a little more tolerant of messy activities and untidiness.

- allow for time. Try not to hurry children up to get something completed.

- remind yourself that giving children opportunities to explore the environment and experiment with materials in diverse ways is an important part of child development.

Embrace your own creativity!

Understanding your own ability to be creative will help you feel less anxious and uncertain about supporting children's creative development most effectively.

Creativity is an ability we all possess to some degree and use every day, whether we realise it or not.

We can stimulate creative ways of thinking, by being a bit more playful ourselves and by sharing our ideas. Begin by following your own curiosity and seeing what really interests you about the activities you have provided.

As you look around children's play spaces, what are the things that spark **your** interest?

Try to ignite your inner inventive spirit and bring your own creativity and flair to the setting!

Think about a time when you planned a holiday or a trip. You chose a place, perhaps it was somewhere exotic or somewhere familiar. Then you worked out where you would stay. Next, you arranged how to get there. Finally, you thought about what you would do; the trips, attractions, and where you would go to eat and drink.

When you made these plans, you used the amazing tool of creative thinking.

We all have this amazing tool for creative thinking. It's called imagination.

Basically, it allows us to explore ideas of things that are not in our present environment, or perhaps are not even real.

The power of imagination

In imagination, there's no limitation.

- Mark Victor Hansen

QuotePixel.com

Using our imagination means that we step outside of the here and now and really focus upon what could be.

Imagination can be used as a very vivid representation of possible solutions to the situations, circumstances, and events that require thinking in a different way.

Being imaginative helps us explore our thoughts and feelings more deeply and learn how to solve problems creatively.

Try to take a little time each day to use your imagination with children. We can show them by example just how much fun that is.

Imagination tends to go hand-in-hand with creativity and plays a pivotal role in different stages of children's development. Children can benefit greatly from a vivid imagination, especially with the support of an adult.

The world of a young child is one of imagination and wonder.

Their imaginations are boundless.

Children adore pretend games and have a natural tendency to invent, experiment, and explore. Imaginative play is based on fantasy and has no boundaries or structure attached. It is driven completely by creativity and fun.

When children are imagining, inventing and creating, something amazing happens. The child sees things around them in new ways and when this happens, new connections are made between different regions of the brain, this then opens up new experiences to the child and to learning.

There is nothing more satisfying and fulfilling for children than to be able to express themselves by having the freedom to be totally involved in whatever activity they are doing and to make it their own; to bask and revel in their experiences. This definitely applies to us too, doesn't it?

By providing children with opportunities for creative self-expression, whether that's drawing, painting, role-play, music, using puppets, problem solving or dancing you are supporting them to express themselves openly and freely.

Some who work with young children can narrow the concept of creativity down to what they see as the 'quality' of the end result. But it is well known that the end result is not so important. It doesn't matter what the child's creative result looks like. It's the process of creative self-expression that will satisfy and delight.

It's good to show a child that **there's more than one way to do something**. For example, there's more than one way to draw a person, dance, build a sandcastle or play a drum. This helps children understand that they can develop their own ideas.

Nurturing creativity

You can provide lots of meaningful experiences for children by stimulating, guiding, and modelling creativity and exploration.

Invite the child to create:

Give a child a list of things to find (e.g., something red, 2 things that are soft, 4 things that are smaller than their thumb,) then use them in a creation.

Inspire creative problem solving:

Ask open-ended questions that have no right or wrong answer. This will encourage children to tell you why they think the way they do. For example, "What could happen if cars could fly"?

Come up with lots of different ways to use an object. For instance, you could use a towel not just as a towel, but also as a cape, a blanket, a hat and so much more.

Cultivate imaginative storytelling:

Invite the child to draw or paint favourite parts of a story. Make a creative switch! Decide that the main character is a bear instead of Goldilocks, or have the story take place on a ship instead of the forest.

Encourage creativity through movement:

Music, song and dance can be stimulating and exciting experiences for children. By providing spaces where children can be spontaneous in their music-making, dance and movement, we can enhance their experiences and they can develop their thoughts and ideas. Encourage children to express feelings by asking them to move as if they were sad, angry, or happy. Have them choose a creature to move like. How can the creature get over the hill or across the river?

Consider how you respond

Emphasise the process and not the product. Ask the child to tell you about their creation. Notice what they discovered (e.g., I notice that when you added more of the green, you got a darker colour).

Offer a wide variety of materials:

Be sure to offer children a wide range of creative materials and experiences. Being creative is much more than drawing or painting. There is also for example, photography, music, clay, paper, wood, water, shadows and of course creative thinking and problem solving through thought and action. The possibilities are endless. It is also important to acknowledge that children need time to explore materials and develop their own ideas.

Keep in mind!

Children in their earliest years who are encouraged to express themselves in creative ways, are more likely to succeed in adult life by developing the skills they need. Whether they are an accountant, a scientist, a plumber, a builder, a shop assistant or a lawyer. They will all be required to use their mind creatively.

Small things that you can do that will make the biggest difference:

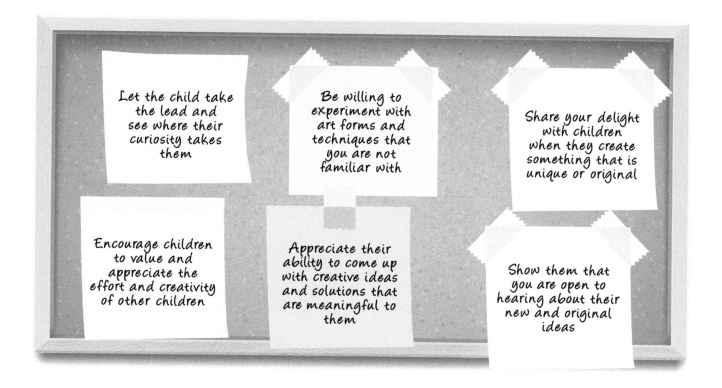

You will know when you have encouraged me to express myself; to be inventive, creative and use my imagination when…

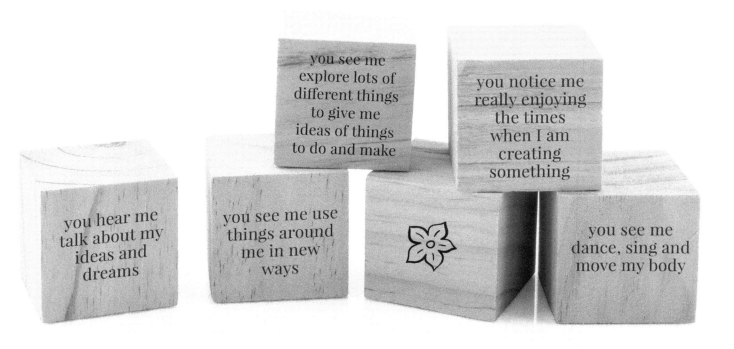

Passionate
Practitioner

Chapter 7: Passion, Purpose and Progress

Chapter 7

"Even though it is tricky I want you to find out how I'm doing, share this with me and help me plan and think about my own learning."

Making decisions on how children are progressing in their learning and development is a crucial aspect of our work with young children and it can, at times be overwhelming.

We know that each day we are making a difference in the lives of children, and we have the power to support progress, but ... have to share and affirm this.

Knowing how important it is to get this right, we are sometimes dominated by a fear of getting it wrong. This can then end up in a belief that we have to document everything, and that we must have written evidence of all our judgements about a child.

Building trust with parents and colleagues that we can show progress means that we can worry whether the child is hitting specified targets, and perhaps focus too much on gathering lots of information. It can also be tempting to look for ways of assessing children more formally so we can be sure that we have the answers to the questions we know we will be asked;

"Can you let me know how they are getting on?"

We can start to answer that question by building on information provided by parents and beginning with children's needs and interests, then we will notice over time the progress children are making.

Difficulties may arise when well-meaning intentions to support parents result in practitioners providing activities not necessarily developmentally suitable or actually relevant to the child. Children achieve much more when their parents are involved, so it is important that you are 'on the same page' and you have a regular two-way flow of information with parents to support each other in the development of the child and their learning.

Informing parents about their child's progress is a key responsibility but always starts with a desire to communicate meaningfully and respectfully.

Practitioners can feel really concerned about this;

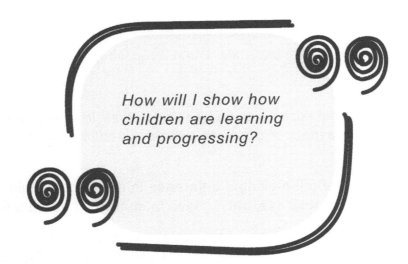

How will I show how children are learning and progressing?

Do you sometimes feel a bit bogged down when it comes to sharing children's progress; lots of paperwork, spending time staring at a tablet or computer screen when you would much rather be fully involved in an activity with a child; taking time out of the playroom to write up observations or to plan for the following week with lots of 'to do' lists streaming through your head?

If this resonates with you, try to take comfort in the knowledge that gathering information about what children know, can do and understand, their interests, skills and strengths do not really lend themselves to checklists of completed tasks.

It is helpful to make a little shift from seeing a child as the individual with needs that adults must meet, to one with strengths and interests of their own.

We can all choose to support learning rather than support task completion.

Keep in mind...

Providing rich experiences is directly linked to how well children make progress in their learning.

Children show us their true level of development through their play, where we can really see the breadth or depth of their development, thinking or learning.

What makes working with young children so exciting, is seeing how children take the experiences and activities that we offer and use them in spontaneous and dynamic ways.

It is of great value to let children show us just how capable they are by allowing them to explore and make mistakes. Our working lives can be so busy and we can often have so many things to do and children to support, that we may be offering children fewer opportunities to grapple with things and find their own way to master new skills.

There is no absolute right or wrong in play, therefore a child's interest and motivation can continually thrive. When children play and have relevant experiences offered to them, they practice skills, explore the world around them and develop new knowledge in their own way, and in their own time.

"The places where I learn should help me to understand who I am"

The key to making sure that children are making progress;

Finding out what they **<u>can do</u>** not what they **can't**.

When we watch children playing, we can find out what they are telling us about what they know and understand, so it is a good idea to try not to focus on what children can't do and what they are not capable of. Instead, look for the strengths they demonstrate and the wonder they bring.

Supporting learning – working together

In the past, supporting children was all about telling a child how to do something until they fathomed it out. Nowadays current pedagogical approaches see us striving to develop a much more supportive role; one that differs from taking over children's play to push our own ideas and suggestions.

"No significant learning occurs without a significant relationship."

—Dr. James Comer

When we have gathered information about what a child knows, we can try to find a way to build bridges between what they already know and what they are trying to grasp. In this way, children can build upon the skills they already have and with the right level of support and scaffolding, they will achieve much more than they would without your help.

We are really bridging that gap between what a child can do independently and what happens when working together; supporting them to solve a problem or carry out a task that is beyond the skill and understanding they already have.

So, this is about offering the right help, at the right time, in the right way.

Sound easy enough!!

Here are some ideas to support you with this;

Give some prompts – this could be verbal, pictures, or gestures to help a child in reaching the answer or completing the task. "What do you think will happen if…?".

Offer suggestions – try another way to do something, by offering alternative choices. Try breaking the tasks into smaller steps to help children who are a bit 'stuck'.

Ask the child for different options – "That's good to do that, but is there another way we could try?" "Tell me about a time when you made one of these…"

Be a real partner – "Let's have a think about this together." "Do you have any other ideas?" Watch out for a chid starting to struggle or becoming frustrated, as these may be signs that the activity is too difficult and they need to move onto something else.

Demonstrate how to do something if that will help a child to understand, then you can then take a step back and only offer support when it's needed.

It is by guiding and supporting children in this way, that they make the most progress in their learning. This doesn't mean pushing things too far or too fast, but instead meeting children where they are, showing them the next open door, and helping them to walk through it.

It means being a partner in their learning, enjoying their curiosity, their satisfaction and delighting in finding out what they can do.

Help children make connections

Children can expand their thinking by making connections.

Plates, spoons and forks are all objects that children come in to contact with. They may not be similar in shape, size or even colour, but they are related. Children make the connections that they are all 'objects used to eat', by gaining an understanding of how things are related. This is done through plenty of practice and some support to help them see the connections they may not have noticed on their own.

This can then pave the way for children to draw on their existing knowledge and experience and feel confident and motivated to embrace new concepts that are meaningful and relevant, and support the learning process.

Learning and focus

Small children are little bundles of energy who are super inquisitive. They often shift from one thing to the next, seeming never to stay for long at any one activity. There is so much for them to see and do.

However, we have also seen how focused a child can be when they are completely absorbed in doing something that captivates them.

When thinking about how we can best support children's learning, one of the key skills that they need to foster is their ability to concentrate and to focus.

When you were a child, like all children, you were probably told a number of times, "pay attention!", the assumption being that in order for you to focus you have to be reminded to.

But focus comes when children are motivated, purposeful and determined - in other words, when they are using their inborn drive to learn.

Concentration is vital for learning something new, but we cannot force a child to concentrate. So, what are we to do?

It is important that we do not see that our role is to teach children to focus and concentrate as this will come naturally but there are lots of ways to increase a child's ability to focus.

100

First and foremost, we have to find ways for children to be enthusiastic participators and investigators of the world around them. Being active and involved is such an exciting process for children and can really motivate them and help them keep interested. For example, getting them to mark make their ideas during play, or perform some of the actions of a character in a story, as you read it to them will help them feel satisfied that they understand what things mean and what they have to do.

The addition of a range of sensory materials can facilitate experiences that allow children to be completely focussed and involved for extended periods of time too.

It's a great feeling to find something that really grabs our interest. There are some things that attract our attention and some which we don't have any interest in at all. It is the very same for children.

Think about a child who is fascinated by something; a particular toy they use every day or a piece of equipment that they can't stay away from! You can use that interest and focus to extend learning in lots of areas around your setting. Look at it as not being about the toy or activity but about using that as a way to develop a deeper understanding of the child and their unique needs and interests.

This is the most powerful tool for learning — motivation.

By knowing children really well, knowing what makes them tick, we can 'hook' them in and then guide their interests by introducing them to new ideas and experiences.

Really hear their decisions and choices and invite them to elaborate:

Children reveal their skills and capabilities to us when they are **fully engaged** in their play, learning, and daily experiences, when they show us three things;

- how they **practice**,

- **repeat** and

- then **apply** their learning in new situations.

When we talk about children being fully engaged, what does this really mean?

Evidence of this will be seen in a child who is ...

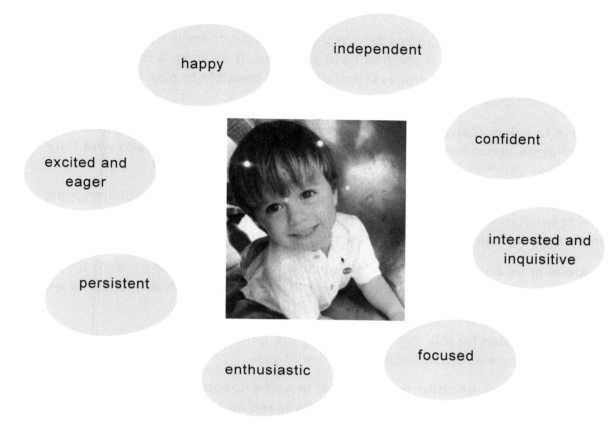

happy

independent

excited and eager

confident

persistent

interested and inquisitive

enthusiastic

focused

Show that you value these positive attitudes by naming them for the child. "I can see how excited you are – me too!" They will love knowing that you have noticed. Using these words when recording progress can be powerful too.

It is rewarding to notice when a child shows these positive attitudes or tendencies and it is helpful to understand how the child planned, carried out, and completed what they were engaged in. This really will support you in providing further opportunities for children, whether that is more time, space, equipment or encouragement.

Remember that we can nurture, strengthen, or diminish a child through our everyday interactions so it is vital to show these positive attitudes or tendencies too. You know how great it is when children see you eager and excited.

Through their engagement, you might begin to see patterns in children's play, such as continuing interests, repeated use of something or choosing to play with the same children. Have a chat with them about this.

This will help you to understand what they already know, find out how they interact with each other, learn about their strengths and any areas of difficulty they may be experiencing and know what to plan together next.

The power of children taking ownership of their progress and achievements

The security that comes with clearly planned out sessions and a more formal way of assessing children is comforting to many practitioners.

One of the biggest uncertainties for passionate practitioners is the question of exactly how to record what children have achieved. If we have a real desire for the child's involvement in this process, it really is not possible to plan for a particular format to their play or learning.

We have to ask ourselves; ...do we believe in offering children the opportunity to make choices about **how** they want to play, **what** they want to do and **who** they want to play with?

This, of course, means letting go of the reins a little and acknowledging that the best ideas often come from the children. They always manage to surprise and delight us with their thoughts and ideas.

Sit, kneel or lie down with children and chat with them to pick up on what they are really up to. Talk about the choices they have made, watch what they do with materials and join in their play.

It is helpful to plan for this to happen during the times that children are going to benefit most from a focused conversation with you.

It is observations of children absorbed in self-chosen play that gives us the most accurate information about a child's learning.

Writing down children's remarks as they reflect on their activities, tells them their thoughts are worth preserving.

Seeing yourself as a real partner and collaborator in a child's play is key

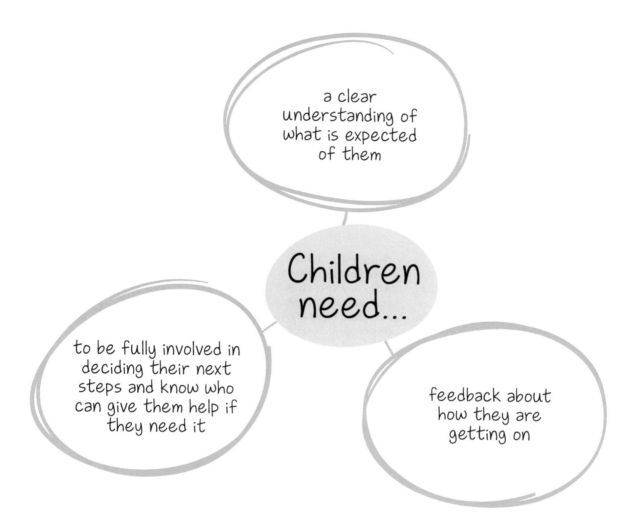

a clear understanding of what is expected of them

Children need...

to be fully involved in deciding their next steps and know who can give them help if they need it

feedback about how they are getting on

It helps if, what you share with the child is tangible

By sharing photographs, notes of conversations and displays of paintings, drawings and other things that are created by children, they will see very clearly, the evidence of their learning. Making those easily available, they can return to them to help make sense of what they were doing and how to develop those experiences further. It is also a great way to stimulate memories of experiences.

When displaying the children's work, efforts, ideas and learning we can celebrate their achievements and show that we value their thoughtful and creative processes. It is so satisfying for children if their learning is recognised, appreciated and displayed.

Doing this in a digital way offers exciting possibilities to share learning with a child but can sometimes be less reflective; can children regularly access and share them when they want to?

Small things that you can do that will make the biggest difference:

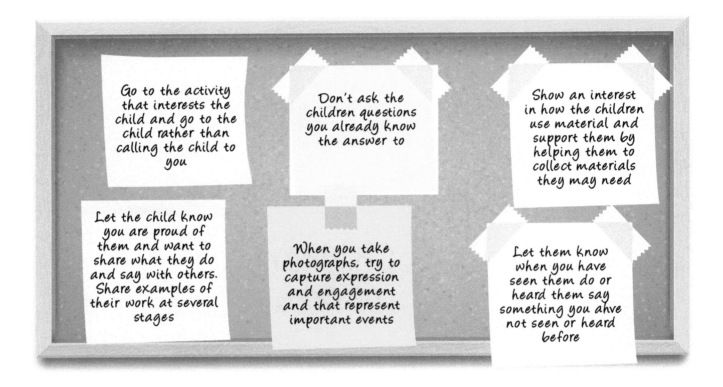

You will know when you have helped me to plan and think about my own learning when…

Passionate
Practitioner

Chapter 8: Keep Learning
Finding your Superpower

Chapter 8

"I want you to make time to learn new things so that you have new ways of helping me learn and develop."

The importance of understanding what fascinates and inspires children is a key theme throughout this Handbook but it is also important to understand what really fascinates and inspires you. Engaging in professional learning can be a wonderful way to not only increase your knowledge and understanding but can also support you to explore elements of practice that fascinate and inspire you. It is essential to approach professional learning opportunities with an open mind.

Regardless of the content of any learning opportunity, your enthusiasm and commitment will support you in your planning to offer rich experiences for young children.

You may be reading this chapter as a student, as a recently qualified practitioner, or are a practitioner with many years of practice. Regardless of which, you have engaged with this Handbook because you have a desire to learn more; to discover or re-discover and that is exciting for everyone. As said previously, 'knowledge is power' and you must not be afraid of the power that can come from professional learning. You can inspire change for the children and adults you work with, regardless of your level of experience.

Just as children can be inspired by you, you can be inspired by other practitioners and this can be through observing colleagues or by joining others at professional learning opportunities. Your network can grow as you grow professionally and the opportunities to collaborate with others can be rewarding for both you and the children you work with.

Understanding the value and power of being responsive to children's needs will unlock possibilities for everyone in your setting as this becomes a significant two-way exchange that results in positive outcomes for both you and children.

Practitioners sometimes say:

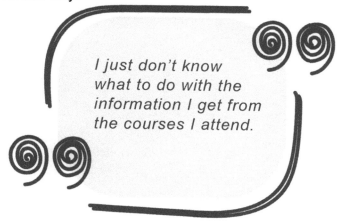

I just don't know what to do with the information I get from the courses I attend.

To get the best out of any professional learning opportunity you may need some support or guidance. You may also need some help to develop your skill of reflection.

Being reflective means that routinely we;

- learn to pay more attention to our thoughts and actions

- acknowledge and challenge our assumptions

- are open to new ideas

- change the way we see things

Engaging in quality professional learning opportunities will build knowledge and confidence and support your reflective practice and this in turn will really help you to understand the children you work with, and indeed the adults.

If you are open to reflection then you will be open to understanding your own approaches and values. This openness to develop your reflective practice can positively influence your self-awareness when coupled with a willingness to make sense of new information.

This refection will build your knowledge and understanding of who you are and how you want to develop and learn. Importantly, it will also build your knowledge of children and the ways in which your interactions with them can be more meaningful and purposeful.

Understanding who you are and what skills and attributes you have, is vital before you can truly support children in *their* development of those skills.

As you play such a key role in supporting positive outcomes for young children, it is important that you recognise the skills and attributes of children and that you also value those skills in yourself as a professional.

Do you do know where to look when you want to develop your knowledge and understanding?

You cannot for example, hold in your head the developmental milestones for all children, of all ages, in all areas of development, and this is not an expectation! What is expected, is that you are able to recognise what you need to learn about, what support you need and significantly, know where to find it.

Commitment to continuous professional learning is a fundamental part of the role of a passionate practitioner and you may have opportunities to discuss your particular professional learning needs. Try to really engage in discussion around this and have the confidence to ask for help and identify areas of practice that you feel you would like support to develop or enhance.

Embracing learning opportunities will support both your **personal growth** and your **professional identity**. As you engage with these opportunities you not only upskill, but you become open to new ideas and create those professional networks.

Be the professional who seeks out learning opportunities and you will inspire practice in others whilst building your own confidence.

Give yourself time to understand and appreciate your own perspective and outlook whilst trying to understand what influences your view of practice and provision in your setting.

How do you perceive challenges?

When you consider challenges, it would be beneficial to try to find the opportunities within those challenges, for example, when you find yourself unsure of how to develop a child's understanding of a subject or don't know where to start when there is a new expectation of you.

Challenges such as these provide opportunities to really enhance our practice.

Opportunities such as;

- looking for ways to have a greater understanding and focus to ensure each, child acquires the knowledge and skills they need.

- through looking out for great new strategies and honing in on the specific knowledge needed to meet new expectations.

It is always helpful to ask the question 'what am I going to focus on next'?

If you don't do this, you are perhaps content to do things the way you have always done or you have maybe simply modelled what you have seen others do. Research tells us that children achieve better outcomes when they access provision where staff provide high quality experiences - but what does that look like?

How do you become the professional who makes a significant impact for children through the offer of high quality experiences?

The knowledge and understanding that you developed as you gain or have gained your early years qualification, can continue to be built upon. Your real commitment to continuing professional development will be essential in ensuring you are the adult that children in your setting need to support their holistic development, and the achievement of positive outcomes.

Your interactions with children should form the basis of high quality experiences for children and you should always reflect on what high quality looks like in terms of experiences and those interactions.

It is vitally important to try to see things from **a child's perspective**. When you open yourself to doing this you can nurture a child's development of their own personal perspectives.

'I can see the passion in your eyes when you have a new idea and I can't wait to see what this idea will mean for me'

To support you to be both responsive and sensitive to children's needs you need to be prepared to engage with and embrace continuous professional learning. Be open to understanding where you may need professional development and engage positively in it.

These are the expectations of you in relation to continuous professional learning and that is absolutely what children deserve. Your practice is always evolving and what is key in this is how you reflect on your approach to learning. Understanding that **learning can really change things**, can be hugely powerful and create so many opportunities for you.

Do you have the confidence to put new learning into practice?

When you feel more confident about, and are able to say why experiences are being offered to children, then they will undoubtedly benefit from this. The environment will then become recognisably one of quality.

Your confidence will also build confidence in children.

Continuous professional learning opportunities can take many forms and will have varying outcomes for you.

You may sometimes worry about an element of practice that you don't feel particularly confident in, which is understandable, regardless of how long you have been in practice. Embracing new learning will support you as you seek to build your confidence.

No one wants to feel anxious, so increasing your knowledge and becoming more confident about a subject, can potentially reduce any stress you may be feeling around an element of your practice. Asking for help or actively looking for signposts to information is vital to avoid feelings of stress.

Embrace a love of learning and the benefits will be evident in your practice and also in your mental health. Increasing confidence through learning will build your self-esteem which will provide a real sense of direction and purpose. Children will notice this change in your professional practice and will benefit from your new perspectives. You can become the practitioner who inspires both children and adults and can lead by example.

Making any changes can take courage, but when you approach change with confidence, the rewards will outweigh the fear and the satisfaction of 'taking others with you' and seeing positive results can be significant and allow real personal growth.

Reflect on the delight or satisfaction that you see in children when you are able to guide or support them in their achievements. This also applies to your ability to offer guidance and support to the adults in your setting where you can be the inspiration for others to grow in their professional development.

Does attending a professional learning opportunity open your mind to new ideas?

Engaging in professional learning can give you the inspiration to make a change in your practice. If this has happened to you, you may have experienced the reward of others recognising and acknowledging those changes. Being asked why you have made this change has the wonderful outcome of making you feel informed and confident enough to say why.

This can be an excellent way to develop your ability to respond with more self-assurance, which is something we all strive to do and has the added benefit of providing evidence of our professional development.

Discussions with colleagues are a hugely valuable opportunity to listen and apply critical thinking, which in turn supports your skill of reflection.

Would your peers describe you as someone who is forward thinking and always seems to have lots of ideas and suggestions?

If children could tell you what they think about this, would they say that the experiences you offer are exciting or would they think they were a bit dull or uninspiring?

What is most important is your openness to asking yourself these questions, coupled with a willingness to develop and learn.

Being open to open-mindedness can be liberating but sometimes you might avoid being more open-minded for fear of not knowing what could happen next but... consider this in relation to young children;

They thrive in a world that has endless possibilities.

You will have observed children as they seek alternative answers or ideas, and will have supported them with this. You too can embrace new ideas and alternative perspectives.

A real benefit of engaging with professional learning is the way it can spark curiosity in you which can then be seen in your practice.

Do you ever feel nervous or anxious about attending a course or event?

By holding onto the core reason for attending; better outcomes for children, your open mindedness to learning will have significant benefits.

> Think of a time where you learned something new about your job or engaged with a learning opportunity and had that sense of 'ah, I get that, I love that, I want to try that'. These feelings undoubtedly support your mental health as well as your practice, and again, can be infectious. The magic of this is seen in how the children you work with will benefit, as will your peers.

Learning can build your self-confidence as well as increase your knowledge and that can only be a good thing! You may well have heard the saying, 'you can learn something new every day' and that is so very true. We are not so very different from the children we work with in that learning creates such possibilities and opportunities. We would never expect the children we work with to stop learning therefore, neither should we.

If you are willing to broaden your knowledge, it will undoubtedly stimulate your mind and inspire you to be innovative and this will support you in the development of high quality experiences for children.

Learning from others in your setting can be a rich and meaningful professional learning opportunity and opening your mind to this can have huge benefits. This approach to learning relies on your skills of observation, communication and critical thinking. Observing the practice of others can inspire you in many ways; inspire you to model practice or to do things a little differently.

The knowledge you have gained whilst achieving your practice qualification, will have provided a foundation for you to grow, and working alongside other practitioners will have a significant influence on your approach to both practice and professional learning.

Whether you model the practice of others or choose to do things differently, your commitment to professional learning will improve your practice; will increase your confidence; will ensure your practice reflects relevance and importantly will in turn, provide real purpose whilst working with young children.

As we aspire to support children to develop critical thinking skills, we must aspire to do this ourselves and continuous professional leaning is the most effective way to do so. Through commitment to learning you show a commitment to reflection and to the children you work with.

Be the person who inspires others to learn, as your enthusiasm and your vision can be infectious.

Small things that you can do that will make the biggest difference:

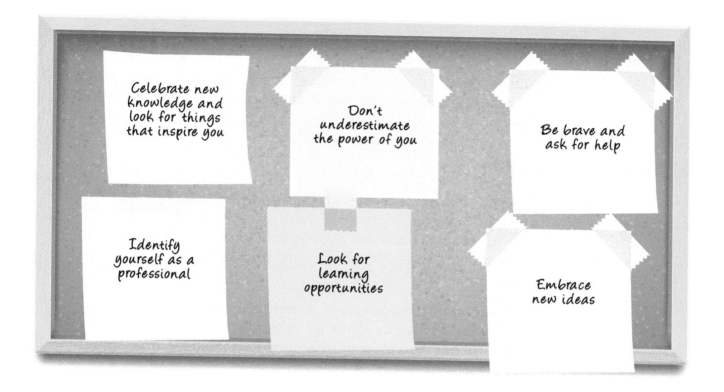

You will know when you have made a commitment to your own learning when you feel that...

One last thought...

There are challenges that all working in this sector have to rise to, but also many exciting opportunities. This Handbook aims to give reassurance to practitioners, to really recognise themselves in these pages and to help them to reflect on what they do and why they do it. Some aspects will be new to some, and for others, it will confirm what they already see in their own practice. For all, it offers an opportunity for self-reflection; to consider different aspects of early learning and to be inspired to attempt new things.

Scale for Reflection

 Consider this Scale for Reflection as part of a process and NOT about pointing out shortfalls in your practice. When you are able to reflect on, and ask questions of yourself and what you do at present, you will be in a stronger position to build on your strengths.

It is important to see any kind of self-reflection as an ongoing process rather than as a one-off occurrence; try to see it as a journey rather than a destination, and as something that is never truly completed.

Reflection is not about focusing on where you are going wrong, it is about embracing a positive and gratifying process that shows where you are on the journey and lets you celebrate how far you have come.

It is vital to be honest when rating yourself, as this process is about understanding where you may need to make specific adjustments to your practice.

At the heart of this process is acknowledging your absolute commitment to making small positive changes in what you do, so that this will ultimately improve outcomes for children.

As with other reflective tools the Scale for Reflection seeks to provide you with the opportunity to take stock of where you believe you are and should be used as a guide.

Scan this QR code to access a downloadable Scale for Reflection:

Scale for Reflection

Consider each of the areas below; specific knowledge, professional skills and personal skills and behaviours.

It might be helpful to think about this as an opportunity for you to use the content within each chapter of this Handbook to support your reflection. As you seek to 'measure' yourself in each statement it is important that you take the time to understand what that statement means to you. You may find a real variance in how you measure yourself and that is part of your professional journey.

A	B	C	D
Highly Evident	Evident	Developing	Requires Development

Specific knowledge				
I have a full understanding of and interest in child development and the ways children learn	A	B	C	D
I understand how to plan and put into practice developmentally appropriate activities and play experiences	A	B	C	D
I can talk about and demonstrate a good understanding of up-to-date information and guidance relating to early years	A	B	C	D
I know what high quality learning experiences are and recognise when children are deeply involved in their play	A	B	C	D
Professional skills				
I communicate well with children and adults and nurture warm and supportive interactions with them	A	B	C	D
I make a habit of asking questions and starting conversations with children, not just to gather information but as a source of enjoyment and satisfaction too	A	B	C	D
I am skilled at observing children and often involve them in planning and reviewing their learning to better understand them	A	B	C	D
I often reflect on and try to improve my professional practice	A	B	C	D
Personal skills and behaviours				
I show enthusiasm and often inspire children	A	B	C	D
I am resourceful, patient and have a caring nature	A	B	C	D
I have a sense of humour and the ability to keep things in perspective	A	B	C	D
I often show imagination and creativity and encourage this in children	A	B	C	D
I have a real understanding of the needs and feelings of children	A	B	C	D

The content of this Handbook is designed to be used by any practitioners working with or on behalf of young children. It has been created to support those who are passionate about good practice in the early years and who are striving to do their very best for young children. It also offers an affirmation of what is good practice and what we can achieve to make a difference for children.

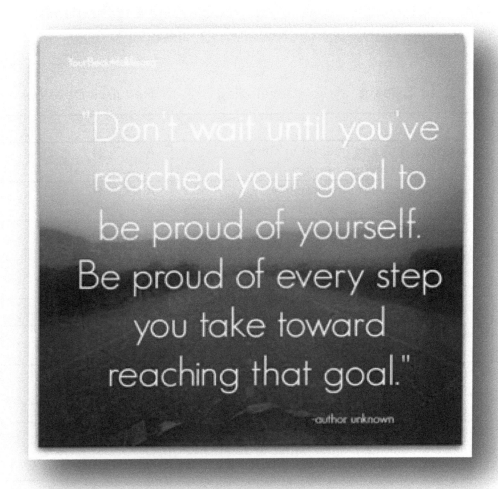

"Don't wait until you've reached your goal to be proud of yourself. Be proud of every step you take toward reaching that goal."

-author unknown